AF481130

SUPER RADIANT

SUPER RADIANT:

A DOCTOR'S PERSONAL JOURNEY

Accomplish More

Work Smarter

Increase Brain Coherence

JOSEPH L. J. SCHWARTZ, PSYD

ISBN: 979-8-218-24463-7

DISCLAIMER

This book is a memoir. It reflects the author's present recollectio[n]
of experiences over time. Some names, locations, and characte[r-]
tics have been changed; some events have been compressed, [and]
some dialogue has been recreated. Although I am a psychologi[st]
the statements made here should not be used as a substitute fo[r]
the advice of a competent mental health professional admitted
or authorized to practice in your jurisdiction.

PROLOGUE

I found my wife of thirteen years stone dead the last day of September 2014, sitting straight up in a hospital bed. Her eyes and mouth were wide open; she stared straight ahead. Next to her were several empty pill bottles, including a prescription for morphine prescribed by one of her doctors. She wanted to sleep downstairs on the second floor of our three-story townhouse we were renting because it was easier to get to the bathroom and kitchen. I was in total shock and panic. My immediate thoughts were self-blame and immense guilt: "Well, you really have done it now, Joe!" (as if I really had done anything). Lisa had had a slow but steady decline in her mental state over the last three years since her father had passed away in 2011.

As a husband I was always there for her, traveling miles throughout the places we lived in New Jersey, Georgia, and Delaware, taking her to pain management doctors and psychiatrists for an assortment of pills and believing she was telling me the truth about her real or imagined problems. It was codependency and enabling at its best. I take full responsibility for that since I am describing only one side of our story, and I firmly believe both partners cause relationships to fail. But when your partner becomes enraged and threatens that she won't love you anymore or may abandon you, this is what happens. As her sister and dad alluded to early on, it was "always about Lisa."

In December 2013 I had slipped and fallen while I was taking down the trash on the first floor of our townhouse after our cat accidentally peed. Logan was a sensitive little fellow, and he must have reacted to the last argument Lisa and I recently had. At the time, I suffered a compound fracture. There was a lot of blood, and the bone was sticking out of my leg! Needless to say, I was in horrific pain. What happened next was mind-boggling. I called up to Lisa, but she refused to help, making me literally drag my body up a flight of stairs to call 911. All the time, she yelled that this was "payback" for me not calling for an ambulance right away when she once fell backward at our home in New Jersey. So, I was thinking, since when do two wrongs make a right? Plus, once the New Jersey ambulance came, her hospital x-rays showed there was nothing seriously wrong. It was just another ruse by her to get drugs at the ER! Meanwhile…that day, I was bleeding with a bone protruding from my shin!

My second wife had a troubled history of treatment for depression and bipolar disorder, as well as doctor shopping, using pain management and psychiatrists to fuel her opioid dependence and prescription drug addiction. In addition, she had immediate conflicts with my two wonderful children, Heather and Daniel, the product of a first marriage dating back to 1981. Stupidly, I allowed her to browbeat me into making sure that she came first over my kids. Visitations with them were always extremely stressful. Lisa made sure I spent only the required amount of time with them during the week and weekends, even though they lived nearby. I think that in hindsight, Lisa couldn't deal with the fact that I had a great relationship with them, while she had a very strained one with her two boys and abusive ex-husband. The first seven years of our thirteen-year marriage were relative good compared to the last six. I had made a huge error against t advice of my wife and beloved father-in-law, Sid, and moved out of state…to Georgia! My sister and brother-in-law had been living in Atlanta for many years. It was my eighty-year-old mother's declaration that "only a daughter could really take care of her" that got my attention. I wanted to be part of my family, even if it took moving out of state.

So, going forward, let's be clear about a couple of things. First, you are hearing my side of this story only. Lisa has passed on, and of course, when a relationship fails, it's each of its partie faults, not just one. Second, for those who know me, I never present myself as less flawed than the next person…I certainly have my own faults. The situation I put both of us in through some awful decisions was absolutely inexcusable, and I take full responsibility for the big mess I created.

INTRODUCTION

Several years ago I experienced a terrible financial setback. I found myself unemployed, exploring some new job opportunities in psychology, the field I had excelled in for decades in clinical and school settings and with a decent private practice. Having received the finest private school education my whole life, as well as graduating from a selective, rigorous clinical/schc psychology program, I found this embarrassing, humbling, and emotionally destabilizing. Starting from scratch was absolutely awful, and I had broken my leg as well, so my job search had to be conducted on crutches. It was a very scary, difficult, and depressing time.

Why This Book?

This book is for all those who have suffered tragedies, losses, and setbacks late in their years. I suspect there are many in our country who are in such predicaments. Despite having many resources, advantages, and opportunities available to them, many people lose sight of these things or have made costly mistakes. Like myself, you could be well educated and relatively emotionally stable but prone to making poor decisions. Additionally, this book is addressed to Americans who have no retirement, who have no savings, and who are broke or close to broke. According to an April 2018 online CNBC article, 42 percent of Americans are at risk for retiring broke. According to GoBankingRates, this group has less than $10,000 saved for when they retire.

Also, this book serves as an enlightened perspective on the members of the medical and mental health communities, who all (while being less likely to admit it) suffer from more burnout than the average professional. Life's journey can be filled with many unexpected twists and turns. As modern life becomes more and more complex with advances in computers, cell phones, and technology, how do we pace ourselves and relieve stress? Many well-meaning parents provide their kids with formal schooling but never address real-life issues like they should. I can't tell you how many men and women I have counseled over the course of an entire career who have tremendous stress and problems balancing work (often two jobs). Is it not interesting that we are also a society looking for quick fixes and immediate gratification (just like all the TV messages suggest), being dependent on pills to relieve anxiety, uplift depression, and regulate mood? And in between all the pill taking, we go eat more take out and more fast food. *Pizza and hamburger overconsumption must account at least 60 percent of the reasons our society is the most overw(the world.* If I am describing aspects of life that are the same for my audience, then this book is right onto some of the problems that affect us all.

What Is the TM Technique?

Transcendental meditation (TM) is an ancient technique dating back thousands of years. Previous research has shown that TM reduces stress, heals PTSD, lowers substance abuse, improves academic performance and graduation rates, and reduces arres and violent crime.

History

Transcendental meditation originated with Maharishi Mahesh Yogi, founder of the organization, and has continued beyond his death in 2008. Maharishi began publicly teaching a traditional meditation technique in 1955 learned from his master, Brahmananda Saraswati, which he called transcendental deep meditation. It was later renamed transcendental meditation.

Maharishi then initiated thousands of people. He also inaugurated a series of world tours that promoted TM. These factors coupled with endorsements by celebrities such as the Beatles and the Beach Boys, who practiced TM, along with scientific research that validated the technique, helped to popularize TM in the 1960s and 1970s. Maharishi also developed a TM teacher training program as a way to accelerate the rate of bringing the technique to more people. By the late 2000s, TM had been taught to millions of individuals, and the Maharishi was overseeing a large multinational movement. Despite organizational changes and the addition of advanced meditative techniques in the 1970s, the TM technique has remained relatively unchanged.

Among the first organizations to promote TM were the Spiritual Regeneration Movement and the International Meditation Society. In present times, the movement has grown to encompass schools and universities that teach the practice and includes many associated programs offering health and well-being based on the Maharishi's interpretation of the Vedic traditions. The successor to Maharishi Mahesh Yogi and head of the Global Country of World Peace is Dr. Tony Nader.

Process

TM is practiced twice a day, sitting comfortably with the eyes closed for twenty minutes. It is a simple, effortless, natural technique that allows the active mind to easily settle down into quieter levels of thought until the most peaceful and quietest level of awareness is experienced: pure consciousness. According to TM.org, there are six important factors to know about the technique:

1. Absolutely effortless: It's so easy and enjoyable that anyone can do it, even children with ADHD. This makes it very

different from other techniques.
- No concentrating
- No control of the mind
- No monitoring of thoughts (mindfulness)
- No trying to "empty the mind"

2. Authentic: The TM technique was founded by Maharishi Mahesh Yogi over fifty years ago and has been learned by more than six million people. It can only be taught by certified TM teachers in a course carefully personalized for each individual.

3. Unique: Other meditations often claim to be the same or similar to the TM technique. In fact, they are very different—and there is no evidence they provide the same benefits.

4. Evidence based: Hundreds of published research studies on the TM technique have documented major benefits for the following:
- Stress and anxiety
- Brain function
- Cardiovascular health

5. Established: Over six million people have learned the TM technique and experienced its benefits—people of all ages, cultures, religions, and walks of life.

6. Nothing to believe in: The TM technique is not a religion, philosophy, or lifestyle. No belief or expectation is needed for it to be effective.

Benefits of TM Program

The program
* develops the total brain;
* increases intelligence;
* improves creativity;
* reduces stress and anxiety;
* promotes health and longevity;
* enhances relationships; and
* promotes peace.

Published Research Studies on the TM Technique

More than four peer-reviewed research studies on the TM tech-nique have been published in over 160 scientific journals. These studies were conducted at many US and international universities and research centers, including Harvard Medical School, Stanford Medical School, Yale Medical School, and UCLA Medical School.

Highlights of Recent Published Studies

* An **American Heart Association scientific st ment** (*Hypertension*, June 2013) concluded that the TM technique is the only meditation practice that has been shown to lower blood pressure and recommends that TM may be considered in clinical practice for the prevention and treatment of hypertension.
* **Decreased rates of death, heart attack, and str** five-year randomized controlled study on patients with established coronary heart disease reported a 48 percent

reduction in death, heart attack, and stroke in subjects in the TM group compared to controls. *Circulation: Cardiovascular Quality and Outcomes*, November 2012, a journal of the American Heart Association.

- **Decreased anxiety and post-traumatic stress der.** Recently published peer-reviewed studies (meta-ana yses and randomized controlled trials) have documented significant reductions in anxiety and post-traumatic stress, greater than those found with other meditation and relaxation techniques.

Recent Research on the TM Technique: Reduced A Post-Traumatic Stress, and Burnout

- An RCT of 203 military veterans with PTSD performed at the VA San Diego Healthcare System found TM to be as or more effective than traditional trauma exposure therapy (prolonged exposure) in reducing PTSD symptoms. A total of 61 percent of veterans assigned to practic TM experienced a clinically meaningful improvement in PTSD symptoms, compared to 42 percent with prolonged exposure and 32 percent with health education. Nidich, S., et al. Non-trauma-focused meditation versus exposure therapy in veterans with post-traumatic stress disorder: A randomised controlled trial. *The Lancet Psychiatry* 2018 5:975–986.
- TM practice decreased PTSD symptoms in war veterans to below clinical levels after one month, with further

reductions after three months. The study found that the veterans who practiced TM twice a day (recommended schedule) had a 30 percent greater decline in symptoms of PTSD than veterans who practiced TM only once a day, a dose-response effect that suggests causality. Herron, R. E., and Rees, B. The Transcendental Meditation Program's Impact on the Symptoms of Post-traumatic Stress Disorder of Veterans: An Uncontrolled Pilot Study. *Military Medicine* 2017;1:1–7.

- Active-duty military service members with PTSD or anxiety who learned TM showed reduced medication usage and an overall decrease in the severity of psychological symptoms. Barnes, V. A., et al. Transcendental Meditation and psychotropic medication use among active duty military service members with anxiety and PTSD. *Military Medicine* 2016; 181:56–63.
- An RCT with male prison inmates, a population with one of the highest rates of lifetime trauma of any segment of society, found significant reductions in trauma symptoms after four months of TM. Nidich, S., et al. Reduced trauma symptoms and perceived stress in male prison inmates through the Transcendental Meditation program: A randomized controlled trial. *The Permanente Journal* 2016; 20(4):16–007.
- TM decreased multiple features of post-traumatic stress disorder in US war veterans, with reductions in depression, anxiety, insomnia, the severity of delayed stress

syndrome, emotional numbness, alcohol consumption, family problems, and difficulty in obtaining employment. Rosenthal, J. Z., et al. Effects of Transcendental Meditation in veterans of Operation Enduring Freedom and Operation Iraqi Freedom with posttraumatic stress disorder: A pilot study. *Military Medicine* 2011; 176:626–630.

- A randomized controlled trial found significant reductions in burnout, perceived stress, and depression in teachers working in a high-stress environment after sixteen weeks of practicing the TM technique. Elder, C., Nidich, S., et al. Effect of Transcendental Meditation on Employee Burnout: A randomized controlled study. *The Permanente Journal*, 2014 Winter; 18(1):19–23.

- A randomized controlled trial on war refugees with severe PTSD demonstrated marked reduction of PTS symptoms after thirty days of TM practice. Rees, B., Travis, F., Shapiro, D., Chant, R. Reduction in post-traumatic stress symptoms in Congolese refugees practicing Transcendental Meditation. *Journal of Traumatic Stress*. 2013:26(2):295–8.

- A meta-analysis of randomized controlled trials (RCTs) found a significantly greater effect of TM in reducing trait anxiety than treatment-as-usual and other alternative treatments, including mindfulness-based therapy (MBT) and other meditation and relaxation practices. Orme-Johnson, D., Barnes, V. (2013) Effects of the Transcendental Meditation Technique on Trait Anxiety:

A meta-analysis of randomized controlled trials. *Journal of Alternative and Complementary Medicine*; doi:10.1089/acm.2013.0204.

- A meta-analysis of three categories of meditation found that the TM technique produced a significantly greater reduction in trait anxiety than mindfulness or other meditation techniques (thirty studies). Sedlmeier, P., Eberth, J., Schwarz, M., Zimmermann, D., and Haarig, F. (2012). The psychological effects of meditation: A meta-analysis. *Psychological Bulletin*, 138(6), 1139–1171.
- A meta-analysis found a significantly greater effect size for TM compared to other types of meditation on a composite index of beneficial changes in trait anxiety, negative emotion, neuroticism, perception, self-concept, and self-realization. Orme-Johnson, D. W., and Dillbeck, M. C. Methodological Concerns for Meta-Analyses of Meditation: Comment on Sedlmeier et al. *Psychological Bulletin* 2014; 140(2):610–16.

Part I

LIFE WITHOUT THE REGULAR PRACTICE OF TM

Georgia, 2007

In the spring of 2007, I entered one of the worst phases of my life. Against the advice of my wife and dear father-in-law, I sold our expensive condo in New Jersey for a large, brand-new home in suburban Georgia. At the outset, this was not a very well-thought-out move because I had no real job waiting for me there. Meanwhile, our house was not ready to move into, so we had to stay at some fleabag motel, which was exactly as advertised. We both woke up with bug bites all over our bodies. Plus, our stay resulted in an infestation of every piece of luggage we had! It was a piece of bad luck that clearly was a harbinger of more bad luck to come.

We contacted several lawyers to take our case against the motel. Finding the right one was also a terrible hassle. Lisa's hair and skin were bitten up, and we found some quack dermatologist who needed to examine my wife "for an extended time." Afterward, I learned that he made Lisa undress completely and examined her breasts and legs besides her scalp. She was humiliated. When I met me later, he said to me, "Oh, you must be her worse half." Both she and I were ready to leave and never come back after this inappropriate and insulting behavior. Believe me, I have met some nasty people down South, some professional and others not so.

Of course, through all this I still had no work. I had some phone conversations with a couple of people who ran mental health groups, but that was it. One woman (I don't recall her name) had a husband who was a psychiatrist and offered me work at very little compensation. This was something about the South I would come to understand: "very little compensation." Another group I interviewed with told me they had to decide between another social worker and me. I couldn't really understand this. When they had an opportunity to get a psychologist, they wanted someone else. All of a sudden, I had no job lined up plus a big house to pay for. At dinner that night with my sister, brother-in-law, wife, and mom at the table, I was visibly preoccupied and disturbed. I just looked around me and felt I had gotten myself into some unfriendly, strange environment with people I couldn't trust and who spoke with a twang. A very real and overwhelming sense of dread took hold of me. It was almost as if I was going to have a panic attack right there at the table. Then, later that week, I managed to locate a regional internet job board, and there were a couple of jobs posted. I was in the middle of responding when another piece of awful luck happened. We both went to get our hair cut at some uber expensive salon several miles away from where we lived. Lisa and I were walking to our car when, without warning, a woman who was in a hurry started backing up her car and slammed into Lisa, throwing her backward onto the concrete driveway. I thought she had passed out, but the car kept coming backward! I slammed on the car's rear bumper with my leg before the woman stopped. I was completely shocked and

devastated. Thus began our second lawsuit and numerous trips
the hospital and the neurologist for Lisa. She was released from
a local hospital after numerous scans and tests. On a nicer note
we met two good physicians, Drs. Ortiz and Lopez, who seemed
friendly and helpful.

After my wife was stabilized, we finally left the hospital.
Luckily, I was able to find work at a psych practice about for-
ty-five minutes south of downtown Atlanta. It was a bit of a
commute, but I was willing to make it. This was a small group,
but they seemed to be active for a while and had a steady flow
of clients. Finally, I had some work! Of course, the drama sur-
rounding my wife continued. She called me at least two times
a day. It was difficult for me to excuse myself between patients
as she demanded time on the phone. In addition, Lisa always
had biweekly emergencies—time to be rushed to the ER for a
resupply of pain medication. At her insistence we also started
seeing a pain management doctor in a nearby town but a for-
ty-five-minute drive away. Since I married her, we had always be
to pain management doctors, and now Georgia was no different
The reception people at this office treated her badly, almost like
they knew her "pain" was more imagined than real. This pattern
of mean inconsiderate front desk workers was a pattern down
South. At her psychiatrist's office, where you would expect to fin
staff members who perhaps understood people with emotional
difficulty, it was worse. I remember one secretary asking why
Lisa was crying after her dad had just died later in May of 2011.
Rudely, she told her that she hadn't cried when her father died!

Her psychiatrist was just as bad. He had little sympathy for our employment situation and even less insight into the dynamics of a couple's relationship. In short, he believed everything that Lisa said or accused me of, despite the fact that she was on a host of antidepressants and mood stabilizers!

Life at my new job was also tense due to the strangeness of the group I now worked for. After a hard week of speaking to clients, the office manager and owner would cut a check for me, saying, "That's better than a poke in the eye with a sharp stick!" The group practice also quickly got tired of my repeated absences from worktime when I was taking Lisa to the hospital for her "emergencies." At one point one of the secretaries at my office remarked, "They should have a room at the ER with your wife's name on it." For the next two years, I continued to work for this group. It was during this time we traded in our Honda and got a hybrid, a new Toyota Prius. Since it was a brand-new type of car, the company had its problems working out the kinks. The car was taking me to work or other places, then failing to start. It was towed twice, producing endless aggravation and stress.

Marietta, 2010

When would this end? If you have ever felt like your world was spinning out of control, *this* was where I was at. Some medical problems suddenly came up for me. I had to have some eye surgery for a cataract (and eyelid) too. Fortunately, Emory University had one of the best ophthalmology centers in the country. Consequently, I had some scary eye surgery there. It was nice to

have my mother on hand for support, and Lisa was also good fo
me at the time. I have to laugh. Lisa was actually taking care of
me, the patient! While I am at it, let me just say that my mother
helped me recover after this surgery and throughout my life as a
staunch emotional, financial, and career supporter. After recov-
ery I was a bit self-conscious, and Lisa started chatting online
with some guy "friends." It was an insanely bad, deteriorating
situation at work, but when your spouse was actively as destruc-
tive, critical, demoralizing, and negative, ready to leave you for
internet boyfriends, it became overwhelmingly bad. Lisa slept in
another room, flirted with men, especially black guys, whenever
we went out and started to publicly humiliate me. I became
more and more depressed and hopeless. This really got worse a
our financial fortunes pummeled. I was asked to leave the psych
practice I worked at due to my repeated absences attending to
Lisa's doctor visits. This was devastating, as I really knew no
other places to work. However, a local psychologist was hiring
clinicians. Unfortunately, there was little volume at this small
practice. Our savings were being eaten, and they could reposse
the car. We had to put our home on the market to avoid going
into foreclosure.

It was really hard doing that and seeing your dream go down
the drain. With the money we got, we purchased a condo in an
old building in Marietta, Georgia. It was one or two rooms with a
small balcony. Most of the residents there were Brazilians. Acro
the street were a few strip malls. I would force myself to look for
work…any work. Some restaurant hired me to mop and clean,

but I could not get myself to do it. Psychologically I was going down, not wanting to get up out of bed. I spent some time looking for work on the computer but mostly shirked and avoided reality, burying myself in a book or novel while Lisa worried and freaked out. Finally, a job came up to work at an air force base through a recruiter who would also pay for our move! There was a choice to go to a base in the Florida panhandle or Delaware (thank God we chose to relocate North out of the South, where so many things went wrong).

Delaware, 2012

The job at Dover AFB in the fall of 2012 was a welcome ticket out of the run-down condo we were living in. Excitedly, we spent close to our last dollar putting a move together to move back North. But this was the USAF, and even Lisa's sister was wary of my success there. The amount of paperwork to work as a federal contractor for the military was completely overwhelming. It also meant getting three recommendations from clinicians I worked with in Georgia, which thankfully I was able to secure. Next was to have all my employment time verified and gaps in employment accounted for. This would be a challenge since there were times of unemployment between jobs. We had no copy machine, so I had to keep running downstairs to the condo office to get it done. Nonetheless we were leaving the South! (Good riddance, I thought.) What would the future hold? We had an auspicious beginning this time. However, our Delaware landlord was gracious enough to take me on my word that working for the government would be enough to assure him of rent without a recommendation from other places we rented from or a credit check. So far, so good. Could this last? Well, the type of "military psychologist" the air force had in mind was nothing more than an agent of managed care. They gave me a huge, long presentation that had to be memorized exactly per form and delivered to each individual military personnel or civilian relative: "I am a behavioral health care provider who will assist you in getting better in three or four visits." (No one ever gets better in three or four visits; who were they kidding?) "Should you require medication…yadda yadda yadda." Completely asinine. As a matter of fact, any client I had would ask me why I needed to present such a long-winded speech before talking to them. As I would come to understand, everything in the military was long winded, with six forms to fill out where one would do, tons of rules and regs, endless paper trails. After that, it was all "hurry up and wait." In addition, you were constantly micromanaged by some tool to see that all your notes were done right. There was more emphasis on "training" than anything else: go to Texas for training, and make sure you are back in time to attend the next training on base. The base was full of meetings, presentations on war, and terrorist preparedness updates. I guess I was just a spoiled civilian, but I couldn't figure out this craziness. All my notes were reviewed electronically to conform to the way the military wanted me to write them. Every other day I could expect a phone call late afternoon that I needed to be "supervised" on how to write my notes. The "behavioral optimization program" had a two-part field exam I had to pass. Things came to a head when at this observation (quite nerve-racking). I missed some key points on the interview to follow up with this patient. Under the microscope like this, I was really off my game. Pressured to the max, I was not performing my best in the alternative universe they call the military. This job wasn't for me at my stage of the game and level of experience. Plus the micromanagement was untenable. The air force and I parted ways about ten months later. I left off with all of them entirely pissed off. I never fully learned the "script"! "Oh my God," I thought, "an insurance salesman psychologist is what they care about?" So where to next?

2013: Down and Out in Delaware

Upon our arrival in Delaware, my excursions with Lisa all centered around her need for pain meds and psych meds. Since exiting the job at the AFB, I was in need of immediate work. So between 2013 and 2014, I was focused on getting my Delaware and Maryland psych licenses and procuring employment. I don't know if anyone can imagine the stress, depression, and embarrassment of being in such a position twice in a three-year period. It's absolutely disheartening. With Lisa's addiction to four-dollar lattes, her $250-a-month cigarette intake, and her prescription drugs, we saw our financial resources once again dwindling. The pressure to find work as well as the arguments were escalating. I was also particularly down on myself after years of education, training, and the prestige of having my own practice to end up like this! There was a lot of intropunitive activity going on in my mind. It was terrible. Then the day came when I broke my leg, and I was stuck on crutches. Pretty disheartening. I have to say that this seemed like rock bottom for me. Nevertheless, I persisted in getting interviewed by a clinic in a southwestern part of the county we lived in near Harrington and whose owner seemed happy to have me. Paramount was getting me on board with all the various insurance panels in Delaware, something she and her office manager were going to help me with. One month, two months, four months went by, and I was not being helped or, more importantly, paid. The practice invited Lisa and me for social events and cookouts, but I was very frustrated with their drag-the-feet attitude in getting me on panels. All I recall doing was going down several times to their office in the nearby town only to find the owner, Joann, completely oblivious, making cookie-cutter decorations for the main office! This whole place had become bizarre and a complete waste.

Through Lisa's doctor visits, I networked into meeting Phil, a longtime drug and alcohol counselor. He was extremely caring and helpful to me, as he was with his own patients. So Phil tried helping me get work as a psychologist at a couple of practices h was affiliated with. Imagine the embarrassment when I showed up at a place of potential employment with Lisa, who had an appointment with the staff psychiatrist, and I overheard one of the receptionists say, "Look. Its Schwartz's wife." On top of that, I know the psychiatrist who saw her must have received an earfi of her complaints about me.

My leg was healing, but the physical therapy was difficult,

and the first stages of manipulation of joints were painful. About this time, we became aware of a cyst on Lisa's breast. She seeme more apprehensive than usual, and I tried my best to keep her calm. We had a couple of visits up North to an oncologist in Wilmington, Delaware, who did a biopsy. The stress between us now was beginning to get overwhelming. To make matters worse, Lisa was in daily contact with her sister Sharon, who recently had to have a breast removed from a spreading cancer. The dialogue of the two sisters, each thinking they knew more than the other about cancer treatment, was devastating to listen to! While I felt very sorry for her sister and the hard times she and my brother-in-law had gone through, I came to dread the phone calls from Florida since this would mean stress and aggravation for my wife on the phone. Eventually, the cyst was removed, but it really was the beginning of the end for Lisa. Her anxiety and depression were getting worse each day as her pessimism about the cancer prognosis reached a crisis level. My wife failed to believe whatever her surgeon or I told her, and she became increasingly dour and scared about her future. All that she could recall was her pleasant childhood spent with her parents, especially with her father, whom she missed terribly but now needed the most. Bad memories of her mother, whom she was also very close to, dying of lymphoma was constantly with her. Personally I felt an overwhelming sense of inadequacy to help her, as I was also struggling to finally find work. Before she took her sleep meds each night, she would let me know that if her news got worse, she would simply take something and *really* "go to sleep." I didn't really take what she said seriously because time and again, whenever I was seriously depressed, or she hea about others ending their lives, Lisa would strongly assert how "suicide was for cowards." Well then, so that couldn't happen to her. Right? I tried to alleviate my anxiety about that.

It's funny how on some level, you finally come to understand how mentally impaired your partner really is after they kill themselves. Lisa always professed that "she wasn't a liar." B years after judging people harshly who ended their own lives, sh did it herself! All those years in denial with her mood changes, angry outbursts, and unpredictable behavior. This is something I pray none of my readers ever experience in a lifetime. We wer between doctor visits when I found her propped up in bed, staring straight ahead. I don't really recall my actions subsequent to realizing there was a dead person in front of me, but I guess I w composed enough to call 911, my sister, and her sister. Septeml 29 turned out to be one of the worst days of my life. Today as I sit writing this, I understand what a long way I have come in my own growth as a person. I suffered a lot putting up with Lisa for many years, including putting her over my relationship with my children. Her death was painful on many levels. It put me into therapy with Pastor Sam of New Day Counseling. Arranging Lisa's funeral was difficult and expensive. After much convincing I got her sister to share a part of this expense. My in-laws were always difficult to deal with, and on this sad occasion, it was no different. The funeral was a horrible event; I had no immediate family present. On the other hand, with Lisa's death, the door was now open for my sister and children to finally be able to communicate with me since Lisa had interfered and destroyed these relationships. But for the time being, other than talking on the phone with family, that was it.

Things were pleasant before and during the service in Philadelphia, but Sharon kept insisting she needed to come to our townhome and collect "her stuff": dishes, silverware, paintings, many things Lisa's father gave to her.

My family and I were well aware of the law, and it clearly stated that the personal effects of the deceased remain with the surviving spouse. It all came down to an ugly scene at her grave site, where my brother-in-law Donald said angrily that if I didn't comply and give them those things, he would throw me into the grave with Lisa. I threatened to call the cops, and they backed off.

I thought things had settled down, but a week later, as I was going out, who should show up but Don and Sharon! Quickly I got out my phone, reporting them and their hostile behavior to the police. Long story short, the officer informed them of the law and the consequences if they stuck around. Afterward I really did not feel safe for days.

Part II

TM PRACTICE AND THE ROAD TO SELF-EMPLOYMENT

Winter 2015: Starting from Scratch but Adding Adva Techniques

In the weeks that followed my wife's passing, I not only resumed my twice-daily TM practice, but I also actively contacted TM centers in the area to obtain the rest of the advanced techniques offered through the TM program that I didn't have. Starting in January 2015, I began taking three- and four-day retreats to practice in a group with other meditators and take courses in DC and Massachusetts for the advanced techniques. By 2017 I had learned all of them. My goal was to establish a firm base within myself to propel future progress. Looking back five years later, I am absolutely amazed at the rapid positive changes in my life!

Shortly after Lisa's death, I was fortunate enough to meet Lindsey, a psychiatric nurse. She worked at another nearby counseling service in Sussex County, Delaware, but my friend Phil warned me not to work there. Then one day a woman owner who was particularly nasty pointed out sarcastically, "Oh, he's single? Now that his wife died, who would want him?" This was the beginning of a series of encounters with some pretty nasty people in Delaware, all loaded with mean streaks and not afraid to tell you. She pointed me in the direction of the NCD, a large mental health practice. This office was a far commute and in

Caroline County, Maryland. Jay and Tom were the two owners, and I was immediately offered a position at a great rate of pay. I took it immediately. Tom let me know to expect "a lot of work and long hours." He wasn't kidding! Starting at 10:00 a.m. till 7:00 or 8:00 p.m., I was booked to the gills. One disturbed person after the next, with bariatric or spinal surgery mental status exams in between the visits. There was also some psych testing a few times. Overall, it was a tremendous amount of work, but the salary I was getting made it very worthwhile. Some patients took to my style and personality quite readily; others had no connection at all. When all was said and done, I saw something like twenty-five hundred initial interviews and was able to generate a steady following of thirty or more patients a week! Additionally there were patients who improved and whom I saw biweekly. For two years I worked this way. Mondays were completely booked from morning till 7:00 p.m. They were exhausting. This routine came to an end in December 2016. The owner had a sit-down with me and claimed he "was losing money on me." In other words, the money he was receiving from me working grueling ten-hour days was not equal or greater than the money he was fronting as salary. I found this a bit hard to believe for a couple of reasons. One was the fact that Blue Cross Blue Shield, the main insurer in Delaware, paid $135 per session and $200 for IOVs (initial interviews). As mentioned before, in two years, I must have done twenty-five hundred IOVs! Plus I saw thirty to forty therapy patients per week. So how do you lose money on a psychologist?

As mentioned, for two years I worked extremely hard at the NCD, often having ten-hour days, sometimes with nine or ten people coming in. After December 2016 I went on contractor status, seeing about as many people but often only being paid $250 to $500 or $800 per month, here or there. If I saw $1,200 for one check, it was a lot! Finally I called Tom and explained it was impossible to pay my bills. He said I should get a "job in a hospital." Two weeks later Tom had a meeting with me and let me know they would not renew my contract! Tom configured all the billing, and with me working for the past five months and with June 2017, it was something between thirty and fifty thousand dollars! But I was never paid a fair rate. In the end I felt empty and cheated.

I contacted a lawyer with LegalZoom to help me. He said after reading the contracts that I had a very good case to get the full amount of money owed to me for back insurance claims paid to me "because the contract reads like you are an employee," and was a contractor. This lawyer got very busy and subsequently d not return my phone calls about how to pay him before or after viewing the demand letter. Life went on for me. Another lawyer at the same practice advised waiting till the end of September when three months were up, as per terms of the contract. Then would "get them" with the demand letter. I felt better about this.

I also was busy with some very positive activities: looking for a new house, working on the note/billing system of my new clinical practice in Felton, Delaware, that I joined, and preparing for my new job working at a school for special needs children in southern Delaware as a school psychologist. Getting and keeping a full-time job was essential to getting a mortgage for my house. Life went on for me. So the first week at being in a school building in twenty years occurred for me that September 2017. Pretty overwhelming, to say the least. I was at a school with over one hundred special needs children and over one hundred teachers and support staff.

I kept recalling events in my life and how I arrived at my present moment. All the meditation, yoga, and advanced techniques continued to be paying off for me. In the last three years, I had made tremendous progress in my career, family, and self-development, and now I was having a house built in Sussex County. *Sweet!* I can't really explain why, but I felt so *good* all the time. Plus I could come and go as I pleased without any partner or emotional commitment.

Then…disaster, just when you think it's smooth sailing. I was turned in by a parent who told the administration that I used the "retarded" label instead of "developmentally challenged" at an IEP, which unfortunately slipped out. I take responsibility for that, but being overwhelmed with about twelve evaluations all at once in a system I was unfamiliar with was manipulative, and I felt unfairly treated by the other school psychologists. Plus no one was available to really help me figure it out! As the days passed at the special needs school, I felt more and more disrespected and abused by the staff there. Fortunately, the blow was softened by the woman who was my contact for Insight Homes, the builder who was constructing my new house. She herself had once worked

as a teacher there and confirmed how nasty the staff at this sch
was after she was "sold out" and harassed. How grateful was I,
knowing it wasn't all my fault things didn't work out?

As my job search went along, I had to adopt a very new
perspective: as my friend Margie pointed out, working in a small
state like Delaware, it was of utmost importance to "watch what
I say." I carry a reminder in my pocket that as soon as I cross a
job threshold, it's time to say little or nothing and remember,
"Don't trust anyone, and expect to be used." *In other words, just
forget about any help from others in Delaware.*

I credit my resilient self for having recovered from this setback. Good fortune struck when I was offered an extremely
well-paying school psych job with a school near Middletown,
Delaware. Half my salary would be tax free! Plus I was offered
a new staff psychologist job at a large practice headed by Dr.
Bob. I was enthused and excited, but there were still a couple of
changes ahead: I started out at two elementary schools but ther
was officially reassigned to a junior high school, along with the
other elementary school. So in the end, I got what I originally
wanted, which was to work mostly with older kids.

Unfortunately, I took violently ill with a UTI. I was in ag-
ony until I finally saw the urologist. But this school district had
problems of its own. Number one, *no* testing equipment. And
if you are a school psychologist, that is pretty much all you do
to make a living. There were several very considerate district
school psychologists who were understanding and loaned me
their testing kits. The pressure to complete reports on time and

attend IEP meetings was mounting for other psychologists in the district, and they couldn't lend me their kits. It was just an untenable situation, and I was ultimately still responsible. A woman who was the lead school psychologist was also adding unnecessary pressure by reminding me she was going to examine all my testing conducted with a fine-tooth comb. She never said hello and had terrible interpersonal relations. No emotion and especially zero empathy. She was ultimately unhappy with my work and not at all helpful, considering I had not undertaken school psychology in twenty years, and Delaware was completely different from the NYC public schools. What I repeatedly found, especially among some men and women in mental health, were emotional bankruptcy and very poor levels of communication. *In short, people calling themselves "psychologists" when they thems needed a long course in human relations*. My relationship ended with the district a couple of days before I was supposed to close on my house! Everything I was striving for was completely ruined.

These events set me back for two months until I was blessed to find work at a high school in western Sussex County, Delaware. *I can't tell you how completely devastated and angry I felt a two failures.* If it had not been for my two friends, Margie and Denise, the real estate agent, I would have just given up. But I was thoroughly determined to leave the apartment I was living in and the difficult area of downtown Dover. The only bright spot was that I did have a great landlord and his brother, who were extremely handy at fixing anything.

Finally, everything started falling into place, and I absolutely credit my faith in TM and yoga. They got me through all this stress and uphill climbing. I closed on my house on March 9, 2018, and was all moved in by March 31. Thank God! I also now had a good job with a good crew of administrators and people to work with in Seaford, Delaware. *After the two previous tries, the third was a charm.* I just felt incredibly blessed to have survived 5.5 years of difficulty, and now my beautiful house was finally built. No stairs to climb too! The day I moved in, a man came walking around the corner with a welcome packet and who was on a welcoming committee. I thanked Henry profusely, telling him I never had such an experience anywhere I lived.

On the business side, I also finally found another psychologist to sublet space from, Dr. Stein. She was a lot different from Dr. Jones, the head of my last practice in Felton, Delaware, who couldn't communicate effectively at all. *Another so-called psychologist.* Instead of calling or letting me know I needed to see more patients per night with him, he emailed me that my contract was over. Ugh! More tumult and stress. But I eventually got my former patients to see me at a new place…I just never gave up.

Now a new chapter of my life was beginning! I had a solo practice and had some stability at work as a high school psychologist. Immediately, I got two compliments from an assistant principal and ed coordinator about what a "horse" I was each day accomplishing the list of evaluations and behavioral assessment I was asked to complete before the year was up. It was nice to have some measure of respect and appreciation.

My New Life and New Home: 2018

At home, it had been a little over a month since I had moved to Millsboro. Going West and South, it gets kind of redneck, which is disturbing for a native northeasterner. People were just different in Delaware! The saying "LSD (Lower Slower Delaware)," which referred to the really slower pace (and sometimes limited mental capacity of residents from Kent and Sussex County), kept resurfacing in my mind. Shopping around Millsboro, Delaware, was very different from what I was used to in central New Jersey. At times this felt awkward and very uncomfortable.

Another development was my mother's passing. Sad, but it was also an opportunity to continue the reconnecting process with my family. Additionally, there were bank accounts my mother had, which were distributed among her children and grandchildren. Now with the extra cash, I had some home shopping to do! I found two nice furniture stores with vendors who were more than happy to help me decorate.

Life Goes On in 2019: Paying for the Times I Spent in

Within this quick year, so many positive things happened. Through much trial and error, I finally had a school district that appreciated my work and was a nice group of people to work for. The journey back to school psychology after a twenty-year absence actually paid off; without this success, I never would be sitting in this beautiful house! In my psychology practice, I hired an assistant who helped me make this very successful.

Additionally, my house was furnished with everything new, and my birthday celebration was only a month away.

As I was approaching almost a year and a half at my high school psych contract, I was eager to stop because the commut from one end of Delaware to another was a dangerous grind. I wanted to stop my proletarian existance. I certainly would not miss the pressure cooker of having reports completed and going over them with teachers and parents. Way too stressful. This wil end, and something new and better will start.

Beating Cancer

Unfortunately I discovered a small lesion on the tip of my nose. My GP told me to get it checked out and biopsied by a local doctor. What an ordeal I went through that Friday! The biopsy was done in a dirty office, with rude assistants and staff who laughed at me after they told me it was probably carcinoma, anc they saw I was nervous over the biopsy. This doctor was also a quack who wanted to cut it out right then and there! His manner was complete butcher/chop shop, and the poor old folks in the waiting room attested to that. They looked horrible! All sorts of alarms were sounding in me as I walked out, vowing never to return. I was freaked out until I researched a brilliant doctor, Dr. Patrick Byrne, over at Johns Hopkins in Baltimore, who was well experienced at nose reconstructive surgery and who worke with a team.

As I write this, I am eight days away from the Mohs procedure of May 2019 that will remove the cancer from the tip of my nose. Naturally, my anxiety is sky-high. Fortunately, my therapist, Brenna Roseman, will be there for my phone calls before, during, and after the cancer removal and reconstruction of the tip of my nose. Damn! I can't believe this is happening, although many people, including a new friend, Bill Kemis, a TM teacher, say it's all routine. There was a steady stream of anxiety leading up to the surgery, which turned out to be one of the most painful (but necessary) experiences I have ever had. Dr. Louise Ng from Johns Hopkins had to remove five small tumors but with three attempts. Between the numbing and removal of the carcinoma, a pathologist examines the removed tissue for signs the cancer is still present in more areas. If there is a wider presence, the Mohs surgeon has to continue removing tissue. Each time this happened, I received lidocaine injections to numb the tip of my nose. The needles had to be about 1.25 inches long. Needless to say, this was excruciatingly painful, and I received four at each step of the procedure! After this was over, they put some heavy gauze over my nose secured by tape.

Then on August 12, Dr. Byrne removed it to perform the forehead flap surgery, used to cover the large defect on my nose. An ancient technique dating back to 600 BC, a piece of the forehead is cut away and inverted upside down near the cornea crease. In a second procedure, it's then moved over the nose and sodded with its own supply of blood. Right now, I await going for surgery number two on September 11 at North Baltimore JHH Surgery Center.

2020: Big Surgeries Over

All my major surgeries went successfully. I continued to stay in Baltimore for a week during the summer of 2019 until the stitches were removed, and I finally went home. Once back, a tidal wave of new patient appointments/requests was waiting for me. Needless to say, I was dead tired after seeing my caseload the first week back.

The year after my surgery went seamlessly well. I felt content, even remarkably blissful, most of the time. I experienced tremendous gratitude that my life was so productive and peacefu Intellectually, my knowledge and skill set at psychology seemed to be growing and getting better at sixty-six, where many peers might think they were slipping. Some minor reconstructive surgeries still had to be performed in the aftermath of Mohs. By summer 2020 I had some dermabrasion done on the nose tip to remove scars. The last surgery was at the end of September 2020 to correct some asymmetry on my eyebrow, pulled down for the forehead flap. This was performed by Dr. Shawn Desai, who took over for Dr. Byrne, who left JHC for an important job at the Cleveland Clinic. It's the second week of October now, and I am healing and looking good!

The Present-Moment Philosophy

With my major trials and surgeries behind me and through the regular practice of meditation, my perception of the world around me continued to change. Certain concepts changed as well. For myself, I found life to be more relaxed, stress free, and even blissful most of the time. Instead of being envious of what I didn't have, or what I had not accomplished, or emotionally engaged in confrontation and argument, I started to appreciate, enjoy, and be grateful for everything I had…*right now.*

So many people just don't get how important that is, except, of course, everyone who isn't here anymore. It's OK to look forward and plan on how to enjoy the rest of your life. But you are only twenty-seven once and sixty-five once, so why not concentrate on the present moment? *I certainly earned enjoying it, based on tl hard previous years I endured. Ha!* While celebrating the now, we can always look to the future, of course. But as the saying goes, "The future is now." Plan for the future, but also take actions today that will help you create a better tomorrow. You can't end your loneliness, for example, without finding some dates. And the journey is often as exciting as the ultimate goal…but where will your journey take you? When we initiate the first step, the cosmos can then take over, delivering your best result.

As my favorite psychologist, Wayne Dyer, used to say, "There are no accidents, wrongful deaths or mistakes…whatever shows up is yours, and it has shown up precisely on schedule as part of the perfection of the Universal Plan."

Presently I feel that no one could have helped me come out of this very hard five-and-a-half-year period than the Creative Intelligence that governs the universe and resides in all beings, what quantum physicists describe as the unified field. And that contacting that transcendental state (the unified field) on a daily basis is key to unlocking, as Jesus said, "the Kingdom of God that lies within us." Going forward I know with confidence that the only requirement and secret to life were to have a simple faith, work hard and persistently at whatever I needed to do, and keep up the TM/yoga…probably the most important part of the equation. How many times in my life have I discovered that the nonpractice of TM resulted in my emotional health becoming completely thwarted? Almost always, this also resulted in my life being an absolute mess. I remember Lisa even once trying to get me to believe "meditation was of the devil" and fill my mind with hogwash.

I also believe after all these years of meditating, one of the greatest benefits of TM practice is the ability to deal with all the angry, misguided, and sometimes hostile people who *don't* practice TM. Look at the news: we see how bad the USA has become with the encouragement of extremism, violence, and hatred. A stressed-out society filled with angry citizens split alon Democratic or Republican Party lines, prejudiced haters, and gu lovers. In 2020 we saw this all come to a head with the racial an police brutality issues sparked by the G. Floyd murder. White hatred and black resentment, attitude, and defiance. Additionally issues affecting the environment, health care, and public safety during a pandemic contribute to the divisiveness we witness as we head to the US election in November 2020.

What a blessing the practice of TM could be if millions of people started its regular practice! *When you are good with your you can easily be more accepting and friendly toward others.* For years of research has shown that TM develops the brain, increa self-actualization, promotes clear thinking comprehension and the ability to focus, and reduces high blood pressure.

Consciousness as a Basis of Happiness: Vedic Know Validated by Modern Science

The TM technique is practiced by millions of highly successful people, including Oprah Winfrey, Jerry Seinfeld, Ray Dalio, Ellen DeGeneres, Hugh Jackman, Clint Eastwood, Katy Perry, Tom Hanks, Cameron Diaz, and more. But where does the source of such important knowledge originate? And how can science validate its existence as well as the benefits derived from a technique first practiced three millennia ago?

Starting in the 1950s and 1960s, it was Maharishi Mahesh. Yogis expressed a desire to eliminate suffering in the world, beginning on an individual basis. What is it like to experience more positive and less stressful experiences in life, and how does one accomplish that? Is it merely a change in attitude? A reconditioning of thought patterns? Or are other techniques and behaviors necessary to reach such a goal? As I have told many of my patien I can only present my own experiences as a guide before they can arrive at some understanding. I try to explain what it is to be more spiritually alive, but often words fail to convey an actual experience. Such states can really only be experienced firsthand.

Happiness can mean different things to different people arriving at that state, and maintaining it under changing circumstances is not something we all can readily achieve. So how does one develop the understanding that "there is no way to

happiness; happiness is the way"? This can be easily accomplis
by the simple practice of one technique, TM, and employing a
mantra during a fifteen- or twenty-minute session twice a day an
entering the transcendental state of consciousness: "As practice
gets steady over time, one can eventually reach higher states of
consciousness wherein the calm, blissful transcendental state is
experienced in all states of consciousness: waking, sleeping, an
dreaming" (tm.org).

Part III

BECOMING SUPER RADIANT:

Enjoying the Health and Emotional Benefits
of TM while Raising World Consciousness

Uncovering the Ultimate Reality of Life: Modern Ph⟩ Ancient Vedic Knowledge

What does Maharishi's vision of life's ultimate reality have to do with work by physicists on a theory to describe a single, unified source of all force and matter fields? *Vedic scholar Dr. William Sands, in his book Maharishi Mahesh Yogi and His Gift to the W* talks about that. At the end of the nineteenth century, all scientifi⟨ assumptions still held that matter could be reduced to basic sets of molecules or atoms. With the advent of quantum mechanics in the 1920s, more research revealed even more basic levels of matter, which were unified at more fundamental levels. Dr. Alber⟩ Einstein was the first to use the term "unified field theory" to describe a theory that unified the basic force and matter fields and provided a picture of a unified source of all matter. Modern physicists now describe theoretical descriptions of a unified origi⟩ of the four fundamental forces in nature—electromagnetism, weak interaction, strong interaction, and gravity. In the realm of science, such theories describe a unified foundation for all matte⟩ and force fields, which are all of the particles comprising the ba-sis of the universe. According to Vedic literature, all the laws of nature have a basis in a unified source of order and intelligence. Thus, the ultimate reality of our material universe can have two different approaches but mean the same thing!

These two approaches—Maharishi's Vedic approach and the objective approach of modern science—represent different ways of considering the ultimate reality of our material universe. Dr. John Hagelin, a highly regarded quantum field theorist and the president of the Maharishi University of Management, has written on the many parallels between Maharishi's description of the nature and properties of being and quantum field theory descriptions of nature's functioning. These similarities have led him, along with a growing number of scientists, to conclude that the unified field of modern science and the field of being, or pure consciousness, are one and the same.

So while we all exist here on planet Earth in diverse forms and expressions, we have the opportunity to coexist with the knowledge that all of us are just a part of nature and one of the diverse parts of creation. The enhancement of such perception begins with the regular practice of TM. As the meditator experiences an expansion in his own consciousness, of happiness and well-being, can such an effect be transferred to the rest of society

Brain Wave Coherence and TM

In his article published by MERU International Group, Declan Godfrey explains the advantages of maintaining coherence within one's own brain while doing TM, as well as the benefits of this effect on the rest of society. According to Godfrey, Coherence is the "quality of forming a unified whole." In TM this coherence relates to the brain and makes it function in a more coherent

way. Scientists look at brain waves and see if they cohere or if tl
neurons (brain cells) communicate coherently. Since brain cells
relate via electrical current, those electrical fields are measured
using a method called electroencephalography (EEG) and can
actually be seen as "brain waves" on a graph. When different
parts of the brain are compared, the more similar and greater th
coherence, the more efficiently the neurons are communicating.

Many years ago, in 1983, Drs. David Orme-Johnson, Nidich,
and Wallace researched how the practice of the TM technique
increases EEG alpha coherence and how the brain starts working better. *More importantly, large groups of people practicing T*
together actually create a coherence effect of positivity, calm, ar
well-being. Coherence is the brain's ability to communicate via
neurons and to see whether this communication is coherent. A
small electrical current exists between cells, and when this comm
nication is going on, this creates electrical fields. After electrode:
are attached to the scalp, these electrical fields are measured vi
EEG or electroencephalography. When put onto a graph, they
resemble a wave on the ocean and are called "brain waves." Th
brain waves coming from different parts of the cortex can be
compared, and when there is more similarity, there is greater
coherence, and therefore all the neurons are communicating mo
efficiently. In a paper entitled "Group Coherence: What Is It and
Does it Matter?" by Declan Godfrey (2020), Godfrey describes
this coherence as resembling a company putting together a wel

---

1   Godfrey, Declan. 2020. "Group Coherence: What Is It, and Does It
Matter?" *Dr. Tony Nader Transcendental Meditation* (blog). 1–11.

site, where the marketing team must communicate its ideas to developers, designers, and customer service representatives. If ea of these team members communicates well, the more efficiently the website will be done. In the same way, the brain is going to be working better because EEG alpha coherence increases through the practice of the TM technique (Nidich, Orme-Johnson, and Wallace, 1983).

While it is possible that TM helps us as individuals, when can this practice also affect other people? In Godfrey's article, he also documented a phenomenon of the effects of a fifty-person group of meditators on the brain waves of another individual. A volunteer was asked to have his brain waves measured via EEG. The group witnessed the subject's coherence when just sitting quietly without doing TM, and it was fairly unsteady. This person continued to quietly sit, not doing any TM. *Then when all forty-nine participants started meditating, the seated individual saw his brain waves become steadier and more coherent!*

Thus, the more people who meditate together as a group, the greater the coherence effect and benefit to the rest of society. This was discovered in 1974 and is known as the Maharishi effect. In an experiment conducted by social scientists back then, they studied four towns where the number of people practicing the TM technique reached 1 percent of the town's population. With this 1 percent of active meditators, it was noted that negative behaviors like crime, disharmony, and violence were reversed, suggesting that the collective consciousness the four towns were experiencing was correlated with increasing harmony and order overall. Moreover, Godfrey's article suggests that these groups of meditators need *not* all be in the same *place.* He cites the observation of Gunter Chasse, vice president of military science in the Global Union of Scientists for Peace, who stated that in studies of group coherence and the Maharishi effect, the best results can be obtained if all meditate at a *simultaneous time.*

Coherence and Helping Your Body Eliminate Stress Prevent Disease

In their book *The Coherence Effect* (2020), authors Wallace, Marcus, and Clark describe how, according to a *Forbes* magazine survey, while the United States leads the world in preventive care medicine, the state of health in the United States as compared to ten other industrialized countries like Germany, UK, Canada, and France was last in the three measures of healthy lives: life expectancy for a person aged sixty, infant mortality, and mortality treatable by medical care. So why are so many Americans leading unhealthy lives? The answer is our form of preventive medicine is inadequate. At the heart of this problem is a population that overworks itself: according to a 2020 report of the International Labor Organization, we work 350 more hours per year (nine weeks) greater than Europeans. In another study, the American Institute of Stress found that workplace stress accounts for 46 percent of all job stress. Also, that stress is the main disruptor of the body's coherence and contributes to an unhealthy lifestyle. Stress can increase the likelihood of stroke by 50 percent, the risk of heart attack by 25 percent, and heart disease by 40 percent.

Furthermore, the institute warned that stress is the basic cause of 60 percent of all illnesses and diseases and that 40 to 44 percent of stressed people eat unhealthily or overeat, lose sleep daily, and account for 75 percent of doctor visits.

Stress is an internal bodily reaction to external events that are potentially stressful. For example, one person's reaction to a stressful situation might result in chronic disease, whereas another person might respond to it differently and easily.

This is where the TM technique can be so effective in reducing stress and preventing disease by increasing internal coherence. A 1987 study reported in *Psychosomatic Medicine* 49 (493–507) found that in a five-year study of two thousand individuals practicing the TM technique, their medical care utilization, including hospital days and outpatient visits, was lower than the norm across all age groups, with the greatest reduction (69 to 74 percent) occurring in older adults of forty-plus years.

Overcoming Emotional Disorders

The bulk of this book suggests how my own personal tragedy and emotional struggles were successfully resolved through the benefit of TM practice. I would like to cite some examples and research studies that demonstrate its effectiveness in combating both anxiety and mood disorders such as PTSD and major depression.

The earliest and most extensive study on TM and anxiety was

---

2   And 3 same reference (next page bottom)
3   R. K. Wallace, J. B. Marcus, and C. S. Clark. *The Coherence Effect* (Armin Lear Press, 2020).

conducted between 1984 and1989 by Stanford researcher Dr. Kenneth Epley and his colleagues. TM was compared to other forms of relaxation techniques such as Tao meditation, progress muscle relaxation, and biofeedback. In the TM group, a significantly greater effect was achieved compared to other programs. almost a full standard deviation or twice the effect of placebo, PMR, other meditation, or EMG biofeedback.

For the sake of brevity, the more recent studies on TM and anxiety reduction include a large 2014 *Journal of Alternative and Complementary Medicine* meta-analysis study combining sixtee studies with 1,295 participants, which showed TM to be most effective with persons with the highest levels of anxiety, such as veterans with PTSD, prison inmates, and those diagnosed with chronic anxiety. The TM group results were superior as compare with other techniques such as mindfulness.

A 2018 article in *Lancet Psychiatry* described a $2.4 million study funded by the Department of Defense on TM and post-traumatic stress disorder (PTSD). PTSD can be described as recalle trauma and the reexperience of a dangerous or life-threatening event such as a car accident, shooting, or military combat event The best therapy for such individuals endorsed by the American Psychiatric Association as well as the Department of Veteran Affairs has been prolonged exposure therapy (PET). This type of therapy involves an exploration of the patient's trauma and thoughts and feelings about it with a mental health expert. Reliving the trauma in a safe environment is thought to help victims see their bad experiences differently and train them to overcome their fears. Of course, many trauma survivors find reliving horrific events quite uncomfortable, and it's estimated 60 to 70 percent remain diagnosed with PTSD. In the Department of Defense study, 203 veterans were randomly assigned to three groups. TM was compared to health education and traditional PET. PTSD symptoms were measured by administration of a clinically administered PTSD score (CAPS) after the training was over. The TM group reported a 61 percent reduction in PTSD symptoms versus 42 percent for PET and 32 percent for health education.

TM also effectively reduces symptoms of major depressive disorder. A large study was conducted in 2009 and published in the *American Journal of Hypertension*, in which 298 university students were divided into a wait-list group and the other learned TM. A subgroup of 159 was also studied that had a genetic risk for hypertension. The TM groups showed a significant improvement in coping ability and reduced depression, anxiety, and anger, as well as the physical component of lower blood pressure. A random control study conducted at the West Oakland Health Center evidenced a 48 percent drop in depression for individuals with three months of practicing TM versus an increase in reported depression symptoms by a control group that took a stress management course.

---

4 "Psychological Distress and Coping in Young Adults," *American Journal of Hypertension* 22, no. 12 (2009): 1326–1331.
5   J. Claes, *The Field Paradigm: 20 Experiments That Can Change the World* (2017), p 134.

Lasting Happiness

In life, like my own experiences previously described, there are unpleasant events that happen all the time. All of us prefer for life to be easy and stressless, free from any difficulty. Falsely we hold onto beliefs that events or experiences such as achieving a goal, getting high marks at school, earning a job promotion, or getting married result in our feelings of joy and happiness. I believe what I discovered in the course of my own recent journe was a common experience shared by many TM mediators: that happiness is actually separate from external experiences, includ setbacks, mistakes, and failures; that feelings of stability, peace, calmness grew within myself the longer I regularly practiced TM and all the advanced techniques I learned; and that those blissft feelings and elevated moods extended beyond my daily practice into regular activity. Most importantly, these positive energies were directly correlated with increased coherent physiology. In 2021, for example, I had the occasion to visit my primary care physician (PCP) and urologist. Over the last three years, my PCP was concerned that my A1C level was borderline, then was happy to tell me it dropped one point. Similarly, my urologist said my PSA level was not only normal but also had dropped a full point! What I also discovered was that the extended feelings of well-being created by my TM practice had no detrimental effect on my ambition, drive, or will to improve and succeed. In fact, after learning all the advanced techniques on top of the TM Siddhi program, I was now running my own practice and living in a new home in northwest Wilmington, Delaware (only seven minutes away from the president of the United States).

Part IV

BEHAVIOR WITHIN THE RELATIVE SPHERE OF EXISTENCE

In retrospect, all the difficult situations I faced between 2013 and 2018 were like tests, some of which I passed with flying colors. Some I failed miserably, and some I had more or less appropriate responses to. With the addition of several TM advanced techniques, I believe I grew exponentially in consciousness, and this had a very beneficial effect on all my behavior in life. Recently over the course of a week, I quickly devoured Dr. Tony Nader's new book *One Unbounded Ocean of Consciousness*, and for anyone who is interested in learning the TM technique or is a spiritual aspirant, the book ranks as one of the foremost interpretations of Vedic science and its extrapolation to modern life. Life is change, and we are all changing, getting older and hopefully better. For practitioners of TM, on the other hand, daily exercises in yoga, TM, and the TM Siddhi program offer an extraordinary opportunity to grow toward higher states of consciousness that naturally affect their own behaviors. *Personally, where I was five years ago in consciousness is not where I am today.* My behavior with others is much easier, often effortless, easily saying and doing the right thing with fewer impulsive or angry reactions. Inside, I am kinder, gentler with myself…and especially more compassionate with others who are not so "enlightened." Do I ever get angry with people in general or people whom I talk to on the phone? Sure, but it happens quickly, and I am then on to the next moment. As Dr. Nader clearly states in his latest book, the ability to grow in consciousness through the TM techniques helps individuals evolve to behaviors that encourage them to become happier, more successful, and excited about their futures.

Many years ago, Guru Dev, spiritual master and guide to Mahahirishi Mahesh Yogi, published his *Satsangs Rendered* in order to guide individuals in their daily behaviors, particularly with themselves and others. From here, I learned to adhere to some important principles. Foremost was to seek the Supreme Se (the source of consciousness) within as a prerequisite to enjoying the highest happiness. This, of course, meant the daily practice of TM meditation. As Guru Dev suggested, "How can you get wealthy just by studying a catalogue? In worldly life, seeking happiness without Paramatma (Supreme Self) is like trying to quench your thirst by gathering small dewdrops." Additionally, he said, "the Supreme Self can deliver any object without ever

---

6   T. Nader, *One Unbounded Ocean of Consciousness* (Penguin Random House Press, 2021).

running out of supplies."

What struck me as most important in his discourses were the references to maintaining correct dharma (e.g., righteous ways, virtuous actions) and behaviors that are said to be in accord with Rita, the order that makes life and universe possible, and how important it was to lead a life of purity by behaving properly with others. Then I thought, "But how can one always be doing that?" Surely Guru Dev, who for most of his life inhabited the forests and caves of northern India, had little understanding of the problems of modern life, its stresses and strains, job and family obligations that could easily wreak havoc on one's own inner peace and also contribute to bad behaviors.

From my understanding of the TM practice, however, the daily twenty minutes of this meditation will eventually help you to do just that (i.e., maintain your inner peace, equanimity, and joy, even while experiencing discomfort, delay, or disappointment). TM encourages behavior that is in accord with dharma (cosmic order) and not adharma (discord, wrongness), the ways of anoth that can be disastrous. Disaster strikes when we become victim of our own actions or karma. Have you heard the expression "What goes around comes around?" or "As you sow, so shall yo reap"? Such are descriptions of the results that come from good and bad behaviors. The growth of individual consciousness and its evolution to higher levels of consciousness naturally accomplish this. *So if we all are going to be successful at the art of livir and avoid behaviors that may result in bad outcomes, we must l*

---

7   Guru Dev. *Guru Dev Satsangs Rendered (1941–1953)*, 2.

the basis of all our actions firmly rooted in the practice of TM and increase our ability to experience true awareness and divine bliss. Dr. Tony Nader further addresses the issue of human behavior and true freedom:

> When awareness is limited, freedom is limited. The narrower the awareness, the smaller will be the range and degree of freedom. It is from the transcendental level that we can harness the infinite power and intelligence of the absolute…and is a confirmation of our supreme freedom. From these deep levels of being, thoughts are more powerful than action. The right thought at these levels can even balance and neutralize karmic influences.

The premise of this book is based on the assumption that there is a direct correlation between the good and bad times in my life, the better decisions versus the poorer ones, and the steady practic of TM. As I mentioned earlier, my experiences were much more positive and successful, with good outcomes when I meditated twice each day. Frankly, I don't think I would have been able to achieve the beneficial turnaround in my life without it!

---

8   T. Nader, *One Unbounded Ocean of Consciousness* (Penguin Random House Press, 2021), 284–329.

Part V

A PRESCRIPTION FOR YOUR FUTURE:

No Masks, No Vaccination, No Pills, No Diet…No Religion, Political Party, or Lifestyle Required

One of my favorite congressmen is Democratic representative Tim Ryan of Ohio. Here is what he had to say about how to heal America and help government leaders and the country through meditation:

> The call for us is the inward journey, to really under-
> standing the capacity of human beings…to try to find
> some clarity. Instead of getting into fights on social
> media, let's take some time, 20 minutes twice a day…
> to go inward. That will then give us that cultural shift,
> the shift in awareness, then engage the world from
> that different perspective. That's the call—the journey
> inward. That meets the moment more than anything.

As Americans we may struggle with economic anxiety or the stress produced from family conflict that stays with children and adults. So what choices can we make? A future filled with anger and hostility or happiness and peace? Behaviors that lead to prosperity and stability or chaos? It seems that our society, as Representative Ryan alluded to, is expert at opinions, person-

---

9   TM Talks: A Discussion with Congressman Tim Ryan by Mario Orsetti Executive Director Center for Health and Wellness. The David Lynch Foundation. June 12, 2020.

al philosophies, and beliefs. We firmly believe that whom we worship, whom we vote for for president, what we eat or drink, what groups we belong to, or what schools we send our kids to must be an extension of who we are and that this is best. Why must my child wear a mask to attend classes? We don't believe in them in our family…

My point here is simple. The common denominator among us all is our basic humanity, and it's our common desire to achieve a measure of happiness in this lifetime. Erroneously we think that the Democrats, Republicans, our bank accounts, friends, family, children, or partners are responsible for our continued enjoyment of life. The constant change of life challenges these assumptions: political parties, abundance or scarcity, and rela tionships, for example, never last forever. Your spouse could pass away, a Democrat could be voted out for a Republican, and you might have to work a little harder staying in good health as you get older. Plus, there are no guarantees in life. Sadly, today marks the twentieth anniversary of an unexpected terrorist attack on our country in which thousands of innocent people perished.

Are you as an individual ready to try something, a life-chang- ing technique that could simultaneously benefit yourself and the rest of society? You don't have to change or believe in anything different from what you hold dear at this moment. To all my readers, accept this challenge and learn TM! You will not regret it.

Best of luck to all on your journey!
Wilmington, Delaware
September 11, 2021